Treats and Eats

Contents

Features

Which language lends many cooking words to the English language? Find out on page 14.

Why would anybody work really hard to create art that people are just going to eat? Read an interview with a food artist in **Art You Can Eat** on page 16.

Follow the recipe in **Be a Cookie Artist** on page 18 to make your very own art to eat.

Who sent hundreds of servants to the mountains to collect snow and ice for dessert? Find out on page 21.

How does food keep people healthy and strong?

Visit www.infosteps.co.uk
for more about FOOD.

Turn On Your Taste Buds

Picnics, parties, markets and street stalls all around the world have delicious treats to turn on your **taste buds**. A treat can be a quick snack or a fancy holiday feast. The food can be salty, spicy, sweet or sour. From a cool slice of watermelon on a hot summer's day to a special meal with family and friends, the taste of a treat can be hard to beat.

The Food Guide Pyramid

There are six food groups. The lower part of the food guide pyramid shows foods you should eat often. The upper part shows foods you should eat less often.

Fats, oils and sweets group

Meats, poultry, fish, dry beans, eggs and nuts group

Milk, yoghurt and cheese group

Vegetable group

Fruit group

Bread, cereal, rice and pasta group

SITESEEING
PEOPLE & PLACES

How does food keep people healthy and strong?

Visit www.infosteps.co.uk
for more about FOOD.

Street Treats

Different countries around the world have different foods. Many people in Mexico like to eat food made with corn, beans and hot chilli peppers. Hungry shoppers on the streets can treat themselves to snacks such as spicy corn on the cob or a stack of tasty **tortillas** filled with beans, cheese and hot sauce.

Mexico

People in Mexico have used corn in their cooking for more than 5,000 years. Tortillas are made from cornmeal. A tortilla can be very useful as a plate or a food scooper as well as a snack!

TRICK OR TREAT?

Do fried grasshoppers with chillies make a tasty tortilla topping? Find out on page 22.

Snack Attack

When it comes to spicy snacks street sellers
in India offer some of the world's tastiest treats.
Snacking is very popular in India. You can buy
snacks such as spicy nuts, savoury crackers
and hot **samosas** almost anytime or anywhere.

Many people in India have a soft spot for sweet
treats too. People often send a surprise of sticky
sweets called sweetmeats to friends and family.
They believe that sweets bring good luck.

India

TRICK OR TREAT?

Is black salt just salt gone bad, or can you sprinkle it on your favourite snack? Find out on page 22.

A street seller balances a tray of snacks on his head.

Many different spices are used to make tasty snacks.

9

Rice Makes It Right

People sometimes say that if there is rice on the table everything will be all right! Rice is an important food in some parts of the world. It is especially important in many countries in Asia. People enjoy eating rice balls, rice crackers, rice pudding and rice wrapped in seaweed. Rice can also be made into flour for noodles of many shapes and sizes. For some people noodle soup is a special breakfast treat.

Asia

1

2

3

4

Sushi is a food that people all around the world enjoy. Rice, vegetables and pieces of chicken, fish or shellfish are often wrapped in seaweed to make a sushi roll.

TRICK OR TREAT?

Can you use rice paper to send a note to a friend? Find out on page 22.

Time for Tea

Tiny tea cakes and bite-sized sandwiches are all part of the menu for a tea party. Teatime treats were first dreamed up long ago in England. People ate warm fluffy **scones** with fresh cream and jam. They made tiny egg sandwiches with soft white bread. They washed it all down with cup after cup of piping hot tea. Teatime is still a treat in many places today.

Country Cottage Menu

Traditional High Tea

Club sandwiches
(egg, cucumber, tomato)

Hot savouries
(chicken, ham-and-cheese)

Mini tea cakes and fruit pastries

Home-baked scones, served
with butter, jam and cream

* All the hot tea you can drink

WORD BUILDER

A young man named the Earl of Sandwich was much too busy for a lengthy meal. He liked his food between two hunks of bread instead. People began calling this speedy snack a sandwich.

England

TRICK OR TREAT?

Are eggshell sandwiches special teatime treats? Find out on page 22.

Dip It and Dunk It

Some food tastes very good when it is dipped and dunked! The Swiss made dipping special when they invented fondues. A fondue is a dish made with a hot liquid, often melted cheese or melted chocolate. Today people all over the world enjoy gathering around a table to dip and dunk bread, vegetables or fruit into a fondue.

WORD BUILDER

Like many words to do with cooking the word *fondue* comes from the French language. It means "melted".

Switzerland

Cheese is a healthy food made from milk. There are hundreds of kinds of cheeses. Cheeses are often named after the area where they were first made. Swiss cheese is a hard cheese with holes in it.

TRICK OR TREAT?

Are truffles dark delicious chocolates or are they a kind of mushroom sniffed out by pigs? Find out on page 22.

ART YOU CAN EAT

In the hands of New Zealand food artist Kim Evans, some treats look almost too good to eat!

Kim is at her work table. She is putting the final splashes of colour on a fancy cone-cake creation. It began as just a plain slab of cake. Kim carved it to make a cone shape and used chocolate sauce to hold the pieces in place. Using sugars from the United States, funky colours from England, gold and silver chocolate balls from Italy, and ribbons from France, Kim makes sure that this is no ordinary birthday cake. It is art you can eat— if you dare!

BEHIND THE SCENES INTERVIEW

Q. Kim, how did you become a food artist?

A. I went to art school in Australia to become
a sculptor. But instead of working with wood
and clay, I ended up sculpting with cake and icing!

Q. What tools do you use?

A. An airbrush is my most important
tool. I also run icing through
a pasta machine, use shapes cut
from ice-cream containers as moulds,
and apply texture with tea towels.

**Q. What is the most unusual cake
you've made?**

A. I once made a birthday cake for an
elephant at a zoo! It was Kashin's
30th birthday, and the zoo wanted
to celebrate with a 1.5-metre-tall
elephant cake. (That cake was for
the children at the party, though.
Kashin ate her very own oatcake!)

BE A COOKIE ARTIST

You can make your own art to eat too.
Surprise your family and friends with
a gift of homemade cookies by following
the recipe below.

Makes 24 cookies

COOKIES

Ingredients

- 1 cup butter
- 1 cup sugar
- 1 egg
- 1 teaspoon vanilla
- 3 cups self-raising flour

Method

Mix butter and sugar.
Beat in egg and vanilla.
Mix in flour.
Roll out cookie dough.
Cut out cookie shapes.
Bake at 180°C
for about eight minutes.

ICING

Ingredients

- 1/4 cup butter
- 1 cup icing sugar
- food colouring
- sprinkles to decorate

Method

Mix butter and sugar.
Divide icing
into bowls.
Add drops of food
colouring and stir.
Decorate.

18

Step 1

Sprinkle flour on work surface.
Roll out cookie dough.

Step 2

Cut out cookie shapes.
Place on greased tray.
Bake at 180°C
for about eight minutes.
(Ask an adult to help
with this part.)

Step 3

Let cookies cool.
Cover cookies with icing.
Decorate cookies.

Dream of Ice Cream

If you sometimes treat yourself to ice cream, you're not the only one! Today ice cream has hundreds of colours and flavours. People enjoy ice-cream cones, ice-cream cakes, ice-cream sundaes and ice-cream sodas. Ice cream has been popular for a very long time, but it wasn't always so easy to come by. Here's the scoop on the history of ice cream....

TIME LINK

3000 years ago — The emperors of China eat frozen treats made from snow and ice mixed with honey and fruit.

The Roman Emperor Nero sends hundreds of servants to the mountains to collect snow and ice to be flavoured for dessert. — **Year 62**

Year 1295 — The Italian explorer Marco Polo brings Chinese recipes for ice and milk treats to Europe.

Recipes for frozen desserts, or ices, spread through the royal houses of Europe. Chefs begin adding eggs and cream. — **1600s**

1776 — Ice-cream recipes are brought to the U.S. and the first ice-cream shop opens in New York City.

American Nancy Johnston invents the first ice-cream freezer. She sells her idea and the first U.S. ice-cream factory opens in 1851. — **1843**

1904 — An ice-cream seller at the St Louis World's Fair runs out of dishes. A nearby waffle maker creates ice-cream cones by rolling his waffles to hold the treat.

The first novelty ice-cream bars are sold, even an "I Scream" bar! Some are coated in chocolate. They are still popular today. — **1920s –today**

Trick or Treat?

Yes, it's true! People in Mexico sometimes eat tortillas with fried grasshoppers and chillies as an extra special treat!

You can! People mine black salt in India and Pakistan. They often sprinkle it on snacks for more flavour!

No way! People in Asia make thousands of flat rice paper circles to wrap around tasty spring rolls, but they don't use rice paper to send a note to a friend!

No way! Many people like to eat egg sandwiches, but it is always best to leave the shells out!

Trick question, true treats! A truffle is a rich dark chocolate. A truffle is also a kind of mushroom that grows underground. Trained pigs sniff to find these truffles so people can enjoy them as a special treat.

Glossary

samosas – triangle-shaped fried pastries filled with spiced vegetables or meat

scones – small bread-like cakes made mainly from flour, butter and milk

taste buds – small taste organs on the tongue. Taste buds detect four main flavours—sweet, sour, salty and bitter. These flavours combine to make all the different tastes people enjoy.

tortillas – (*tor TEE yuhz*) a type of round, thin flat bread made from corn or flour dough

Index

Discussion Starters

1   It is important for people to eat a mix of foods from the six different food groups. Why do you think eating a balanced diet helps people stay healthy and strong? What happens if we eat too much or too little of one kind of food?

2   If you were planning to have a party for your friends, what foods would you include on the menu? How would you design your menu?

3   Name some of the countries mentioned in this book. Which foods do people in these countries like? Which foods would you like to try?